THE LITTLE BOOK OF

JANE AUSTEN

Published by OH!
20 Mortimer Street
London W1T 3JW

ISBN 978-1-80069-023-3

Compiled by: Laura Doulton
Editorial: Stella Caldwell
Project manager: Russell Porter
Design: Tony Seddon
Production: Freencky Portas

A CIP catalogue record for this book is available from the British Library

Printed in Dubai

10 9 8 7 6 5 4 3 2 1

THE LITTLE BOOK OF
JANE AUSTEN

A WITTY COLLECTION OF
UNIVERSALLY ACKNOWLEDGED TRUTHS

with original illustrations by
C. E. BROCK and HUGH THOMPSON

CONTENTS

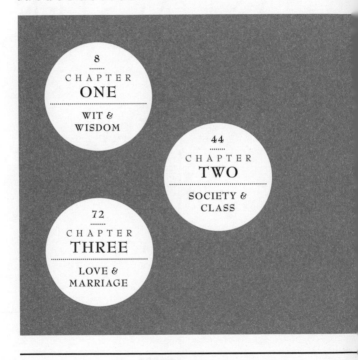

INTRODUCTION

More than over 200 years after her death – in 1817, at the age of 45 – Jane Austen prevails as one of the world's most-loved and widely read English writers. Her six major novels are considered literary classics and remain as popular as they ever were.

Jane's novels reflect the world she herself inhabited and provide a fascinating insight to middle- and upper-class Georgian society. Romance is a notable theme of all the author's works, but the tumultuous path to successful matrimony and the social standing of women in the early nineteenth century provide a strong and serious undercurrent.

Arguably, Jane's social commentaries are as relevant today as when her novels were first published. She mastered the art of subtle irony, making witty digs at the ridiculous, and demonstrating a keen understanding of human behaviour – at both its best and worst. She pioneered a new style of writing, and her works have been hailed for their fictional realism, a stark contrast to other novels of her time.

Jane's remarkable contribution to English literature was not recognised during her own lifetime, however. Just as the heroines in her stories battled against the constraints imposed by society, she too experienced the limitations of being a woman and was compelled to publish her work anonymously. It was not until two of her books – *Northanger Abbey* and *Persuasion* – were published posthumously, that her brother publicly acknowledged her as the author of all six works. And it was only towards the middle of the nineteenth century that Jane's novels began to receive literary acclaim.

Gracing the pages of this Little Book are some of the finest lines ever crafted in the English language. More than two centuries old, these intelligent insights, caustic asides and wry observations – taken from Jane's novels as well as letters to people such as her sister, Cassandra, and her niece Fanny Knight – continue to sparkle with intelligence, wit and charm.

CHAPTER
ONE

WIT
& WISDOM

With her keen understanding
of human nature, Jane Austen
blended wise words with
wicked wit to stir our hearts and
poke fun at the ridiculous…

"Wisdom is better than wit, and in the long run will certainly have the laugh on her side."

Jane Austen in a letter to
her niece, Fanny Knight, 18 November 1814

> ## "For what do we live, but to make sport for our neighbours, and laugh at them in our turn?"

Mr Bennet to Elizabeth Bennet,
Pride and Prejudice, 1813

"Know your own happiness. Want for nothing but patience – or give it a more fascinating name: Call it hope."

Mrs Dashwood to Edward Ferrars,
Sense and Sensibility, 1811

I have found you out in spite of all your tricks.

An illustration from Sense and Sensibility *(Macmillan & Co, 1896)*

Jane Austen was born in
1775 in the English village of
Steventon, in Hampshire.

She was the seventh of
eight children, with one older
sister and six brothers.

> "I am sorry to tell you that I am getting very extravagant, and spending all my money, and, what is worse for you, I have been spending yours too..."

Jane Austen in a letter to her sister,
Cassandra, 18 April 1811

"There is no charm equal to tenderness of heart," said she afterwards to herself. "There is nothing to be compared to it."

Emma Woodhouse,
Emma, 1815

"A large income is the best recipe for happiness I ever heard of."

Fanny Price to Edmund Bertram,
Mansfield Park, 1814

Well! This is brilliant indeed!
An illustration from Emma *(Macmillan & Co, 1896)*

"**V**anity working on a
weak head, produces every sort
of mischief."

Mr Knightley to Emma Woodhouse,
Emma, 1815

"What one means one day, you know, one may not mean the next. Circumstances change, opinions alter."

Isabella Thorpe to Catherine Morland,
Northanger Abbey, 1817

Jane's father, George Austen,
was an Oxford-educated clergyman
who came from a long line of
successful wool merchants — although
the family's significant wealth had
dwindled by the time he was born.

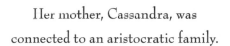

Her mother, Cassandra, was
connected to an aristocratic family.

"How quick come the reasons for approving what we like!"

Persuasion, 1817

"

...there is something so amiable in the prejudices of a young mind, that one is sorry to see them give way to the reception of more general opinions."

Colonel Brandon to Elinor Dashwood,
Sense and Sensibility, 1811

"An unhappy alternative is before you, Elizabeth. From this day you must be a stranger to one of your parents. Your mother will never see you again if you do not marry Mr Collins, and I will never see you again if you do."

Mr Bennet to Elizabeth Bennet,
Pride and Prejudice, 1813

You must come and make Lizzy marry Mr Collins.

An illustration from Pride and Prejudice *(Macmillan & Co, 1895)*

"One cannot have too large a party. A large party secures its own amusement."

Mr Weston to Emma Woodhouse,
Emma, 1815

"**I** will not say that your mulberry-trees are dead, but I am afraid they are not alive."

Jane Austen in a letter to her sister,
Cassandra, 31 May 1811

In 1783, Jane and her older sister, Cassandra, were sent to a boarding school in Oxford (which subsequently moved to Southampton) at the respective ages of seven and ten.

The girls later attended another school in Reading, but this formal education came to an end in 1786 when Jane was eleven.

"One man's style must not be the rule of another's."

Mr Knightley to Emma Woodhouse,
Emma, 1815

"One does not love a place the less for having suffered in it, unless it has been all suffering, nothing but suffering..."

Anne Elliott,
Persuasion, 1817

"People always live forever when there is an annuity to be paid them; and she is very stout and healthy, and hardly forty."

Fanny Dashwood to her husband,
John Dashwood, on deciding how much income
to provide for his father's widow,
Sense and Sensibility, 1811

"There will be little rubs and disappointments everywhere, and we are all apt to expect too much; but then, if one scheme of happiness fails, human nature turns to another; if the first calculation is wrong, we make a second better: we find comfort somewhere…"

Mrs Grant to Mary Crawford on love and marriage, *Mansfield Park*, 1814

While boarding away in Southampton, Jane and her sister, Cassandra, contracted typhus, which had been brought over by British troops returning to the naval port from Gibraltar.

Jane became dangerously ill, and nearly died. It took a full year for her to make a complete recovery.

There are people who the more you do for them, the less they will do for themselves.

Emma, 1815

"Let me know when you begin the new tea, and the new white wine. My present elegancies have not yet made me indifferent to such matters. I am still a cat if I see a mouse."

Jane Austen in a letter to her sister,
Cassandra, 23 September 1813

You mean to frighten me, Mr Darcy.

An illustration from Pride and Prejudice *(Macmillan & Co, 1895)*

"

...one cannot be always laughing at a man without now and then stumbling on something witty."

Elizabeth Bennet to Jane Bennet,
Pride and Prejudice, 1813

"Why not seize the pleasure at once? — How often is happiness destroyed by preparation, foolish preparation!"

Frank Churchill to Emma Woodhouse,
Emma, 1815

"We have all a better guide in ourselves, if we would attend to it, than any other person can be."

Henry Crawford to Fanny Price,
Mansfield Park, 1814

"I must learn to brook being happier than I deserve."

Captain Wentworth
after winning Anne Elliot's heart,
Persuasion, 1817

Jane furthered her education
through reading, encouraged
by her father. She was said to find
great comfort in the extensive family
library and was an avid reader.

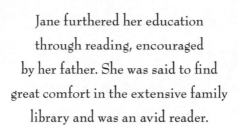

The Austens loved the arts, and
often read out loud to one another
and performed plays.

"What is right to be done,
cannot be done too soon."

Mr Weston,
Emma, 1815

"**Y**our silence on the subject of our ball makes me suppose your curiosity too great for words."

Jane Austen in a letter to her sister,
Cassandra, 24 January 1809

CHAPTER
TWO

SOCIETY & CLASS

From the importance
of social rank to views on
etiquette, education
and morality, Jane Austen's
characters provide a
fascinating glimpse into
Georgian society.

"Another stupid party last night; perhaps if larger they might be less intolerable, but here there were only just enough to make one card-table, with six people to look on and talk nonsense to each other."

Jane Austen in a letter to her sister,
Cassandra, 12 May 1801

"**W**e do not look in great cities for our best morality."

Edmund Bertram to Mary Crawford,
Mansfield Park, 1814

"**H**ere I am once more in this scene of dissipation and vice, and I begin already to find my morals corrupted."

Jane Austen in a letter to her sister, Cassandra,
on arriving in London, August 1796

Jane's flair for writing emerged
at the age of seven when she began
penning poems and stories that she
shared with family and friends.
Her juvenile writing was comical
and often included parodies of
popular novels of the time.

Many of her stories featured
sexual misdemeanours,
drunkenness or even murder!

Lady Middleton was equally pleased with Mrs Dashwood. There was a kind of cold-hearted selfishness on both sides, which mutually attracted them; and they sympathised with each other in an insipid propriety of demeanour, and a general want of understanding.

Sense and Sensibility, 1811

"**O**ne half of the world cannot understand the pleasures of the other."

Emma Woodhouse to Mr Woodhouse,
Emma, 1815

If I were as rich as Mr Darcy, I would keep a
pack of foxhounds, and drink a bottle of wine every day.

An illustration from Pride and Prejudice *(Macmillan & Co, 1895)*

"His character was decided. He was the proudest, most disagreeable man in the world, and everybody hoped that he would never come there again. Amongst the most violent against him was Mrs Bennet, whose dislike of his general behaviour was sharpened into particular resentment by his having slighted one of her daughters."

On first impressions of Mr Darcy at a ball,
Pride and Prejudice, 1813

"I speak what appears to me the general opinion; and where an opinion is general, it is usually correct."

Mary Crawford to Edmund Bertram,
Mansfield Park, 1814

The Mr Musgroves had their own game to guard, and to destroy, their own horses, dogs, and newspapers to engage them; and the females were fully occupied in all the other common subjects of housekeeping, neighbours, dress, dancing, and music.

On the roles of men and women,
Persuasion, 1817

"Is this to be endured! But it must not, shall not be. If you were sensible of your own good, you would not wish to quit the sphere in which you have been brought up."

"In marrying your nephew, I should not consider myself as quitting that sphere. He is a gentleman; I am a gentleman's daughter; so far we are equal."

Lady Catherine de Bourgh and Elizabeth Bennet,
Pride and Prejudice, 1813

Miss Bennet, I insist on being satisfied.

An illustration from Pride and Prejudice *(Macmillan & Co, 1895)*

"Give a girl an education and introduce her properly into the world, and ten to one she has the means of settling well, without further expense to anybody."

Mrs Norris to Sir Thomas Bertram,
Mansfield Park, 1814

He was not an ill-disposed young man, unless to be rather cold hearted and rather selfish is to be ill-disposed: but he was, in general, well respected; for he conducted himself with propriety in the discharge of his ordinary duties.

On John Dashwood,
Sense and Sensibility, 1811

Four of Jane's six novels
were published in her lifetime,
though anonymously.

At the time, writing for profit
was not considered a ladylike
pursuit. However, her family
encouraged her writing
and her brother Henry helped her
to negotiate with a publisher.

Human nature is so well disposed towards those who are in interesting situations, that a young person, who either marries or dies, is sure of being kindly spoken of.

Emma, 1815

"

…it will, I believe, be everywhere found, that as the clergy are, or are not what they ought to be, so are the rest of the nation."

Edmund Bertram,
Mansfield Park, 1814

To flatter and follow others, without being flattered and followed in turn, is but a state of half enjoyment.

Persuasion, 1817

With all the eagerness compatible with anxious elegance.

An illustration from Persuasion (Macmillan & Co, 1897)

Jane's first published novel,
Sense and Sensibility,
had "By a lady" on the title page.

The following three novels were
billed as "by the Author of *Sense and
Sensibility*". *Northanger Abbey* and
Persuasion were published after Jane's
death with a note identifying her
as the author of all six novels for
the first time.

The business of her life was to get her daughters married; its solace was visiting and news.

On Mrs Bennet,
Pride and Prejudice, 1813

A lady, without a family, was the very best preserver of furniture in the world.

Persuasion, 1817

"She has the reputation of being remarkably sensible and clever; but I rather believe she derives part of her abilities from her rank and fortune, part from her authoritative manner, and the rest from the pride for her nephew, who chooses that every one connected with him should have an understanding of the first class."

Mr Wickham to Elizabeth Bennet on
Lady Catherine de Bourgh, *Pride and Prejudice*, 1813

Jane often referred to
her novels as her "children".

In letters to her sister, Cassandra,
she described *Pride and Prejudice*
as her "darling child", and of
Sense and Sensibility she wrote,
"I can no more forget it
than a mother can forget her
sucking child".

"It is very difficult for
the prosperous to be humble."

Frank Churchill in a letter to Mrs Weston,
Emma, 1815

"My idea of good company, Mr Elliot, is the company of clever, well-informed people, who have a great deal of conversation; that is what I call good company."

"You are mistaken," said he gently, "that is not good company; that is the best. Good company requires only birth, education, and manners..."

Mrs Weston and Mr Elliot,
Emma, 1815

....

CHAPTER

THREE

LOVE & MARRIAGE

Jane Austen may not
have married but
she certainly understood
matters of the heart.

From the pressure to
marry well or "the misery of
being bound without love",
to the highs and lows of
falling in love, her novels
capture it all...

It is a truth universally acknowledged, that a single man in possession of a good fortune, must be in want of a wife.

Pride and Prejudice, 1813

> **"S**he is tolerable; but not handsome enough to tempt me.**"**

Mr Darcy on Elizabeth Bennet,
Pride and Prejudice, 1813

"The more I know of the world, the more I am convinced that I shall never see a man whom I can really love. I require so much!"

Marianne Dashwood to her mother, Mrs Dashwood, *Sense and Sensibility*, 1811

At that moment she first perceived him.

An illustration from Sense and Sensibility *(Macmillan & Co, 1896)*

"

…matrimony and dancing…
in both, man has the advantage of
choice, women only the power
of refusal."

Henry Tilney to Catherine Morland,
Northanger Abbey, 1817

Jane enjoyed drinking beer
and knew how to brew it herself.
Apparently, her speciality was
spruce beer, made with molasses to
give it a sweeter taste.

At the time, brewing beer was
considered a normal household duty
for women — and beer was
often a safer option than drinking
untreated water!

Jane's little-known brother George is thought to have suffered from epilepsy and learning difficulties. He was sent away to be looked after by a family who lived in Monk Sherborne.

The Austens made financial provision for him and visited him regularly, but he was largely omitted from any family records.

"Esteem him! Like him! Cold-hearted Elinor! Oh! Worse than cold-hearted! Ashamed of being otherwise. Use those words again, and I will leave the room this moment."

Marianne Dashwood to Elinor Dashwood, *Sense and Sensibility*, 1811

"In vain have I struggled. It will not do. My feelings will not be repressed. You must allow me to tell you how ardently I admire and love you."

Mr Darcy to Elizabeth Bennet,
Pride and Prejudice, 1813

You must allow me to tell you how ardently I admire and love you.

An illustration from Pride and Prejudice *(Macmillan & Co, 1895)*

"There are such beings in the world, perhaps one in a thousand, as the creature you and I should think perfection, where grace and spirit are united to worth, where the manners are equal to the heart and understanding; but such a person may not come in your way, or, if he does, he may not be the eldest son of a man of fortune, the near relation of your particular friend and belonging to your own county."

Jane Austen in a letter to her niece Fanny Knight,
18 November 1814

"**Y**ou pierce my soul. I am half agony, half hope… I have loved none but you."

Captain Wentworth to Anne Elliot in a letter,
Persuasion, 1817

She was feeling, thinking, trembling about everything; agitated, happy, miserable, infinitely obliged, absolutely angry.

Fanny Price's response to
Henry Crawford's declaration of love,
Mansfield Park, 1814

Sitting under trees with Fanny.

An illustration from Mansfield Park *(Macmillan & Co, 1902)*

"

...beware how you give your heart."

James Morland in a letter to his sister,
Catherine Morland,
Northanger Abbey, 1817

Jane wrote extensively about
love and marriage in all her novels,
but never found true love herself.

Around the age of twenty-one, she
wrote letters to Cassandra referring
to her flirtation with a young trainee
barrister, Tom Lefroy. Tom's family
are thought to have intervened
and sent him away because they did
not consider Jane a good
enough match.

Despite never marrying, Jane did become engaged for one night at the age of twenty-seven. The man in question was Harris Bigg-Wither, the brother of a friend.

He was a wealthy man, so the match would have brought security to Jane and her ageing parents. However, the following morning she changed her mind and rejected his proposal.

"It is not time or opportunity that is to determine intimacy; it is disposition alone. Seven years would be insufficient to make some people acquainted with each other, and seven days are more than enough for others."

Marianne Dashwood to Elinor Dashwood,
Sense and Sensibility, 1811

She was of course only too good for him; but as nobody minds having what is too good for them, he was very steadily earnest in the pursuit of the blessing, and it was not possible that encouragement from her should be long wanting.

On Fanny Price and Edmund Bertram,
Mansfield Park, 1814

"

...when the romantic
refinements of a young mind
are obliged to give way, how
frequently are they succeeded by
such opinions as are but too
common and too dangerous!"

Colonel Brandon on unrequited love,
Sense and Sensibility, 1811

"In spite of your manifold attractions, it is by no means certain that another offer of marriage may ever be made you… As I must therefore conclude that you are not serious in your rejection of me, I shall choose to attribute it to your wish of increasing my love by suspense, according to the usual practice of elegant females."

Mr Collins to Elizabeth Bennet
after she refuses his marriage proposal,
Pride and Prejudice, 1813

Almost as soon as I entered the house
I singled you out as the companion of my future life.

An illustration from Pride and Prejudice *(Macmillan & Co, 1895)*

"If I could but know his heart, everything would become easy."

Marianne Dashwood to Elinor Dashwood
on John Willoughby,
Sense and Sensibility, 1811

"Where the heart is really attached, I know very well how little one can be pleased with the attention of anybody else."

Isabella Thorpe to Catherine Morland,
Northanger Abbey, 1817

Jane had a sweet tooth.
In a letter to her sister, Cassandra,
in 1808, she wrote, "You know
how interesting the purchase of
a sponge-cake is to me". She also
became partial to Bath buns while
living in the city.

In her letters, there are many
references to meals eaten and the cost
of provisions as prices rose and fell
during the Anglo-French War.

"**I**f I was wrong in yielding to persuasion once, remember that it was to persuasion exerted on the side of safety, not of risk. When I yielded, I thought it was to duty, but no duty could be called in aid here. In marrying a man indifferent to me, all risk would have been incurred, and all duty violated."

Anne Elliot to Captain Wentworth,
Persuasion, 1817

"There is safety in reserve, but no attraction. One cannot love a reserved person."

Frank Churchill to Emma Woodhouse,
Emma, 1815

He has asked her, my dear.

An illustration from Emma (Macmillan & Co, 1896)

**"Could there be finer symptoms?
Is not general incivility the very
essence of love?"**

Elizabeth Bennet to her aunt Mrs Gardiner,
Pride and Prejudice, 1813

"I cannot fix on the hour, or the spot, or the look, or the words, which laid the foundation. It is too long ago. I was in the middle before I knew that I had begun."

Mr Darcy to Elizabeth Bennet,
describing when and how he fell in love with her,
Pride and Prejudice, 1813

Happiness in marriage is entirely a matter of chance.

Pride and Prejudice, 1813

She held out her hand.

An illustration from Pride and Prejudice *(Macmillan & Co, 1895)*

CHAPTER
FOUR

MEN & WOMEN

At a time when men
and women played vastly
different roles in society,
Jane Austen was
well ahead of her time –
and determined to make
a point!

"**W**herever you are you should always be contented, but especially at home, because there you must spend the most of your time."

Mrs Morland to her daughter, Catherine,
Northanger Abbey, 1817

Jane often stayed with her brother Edward who had been "adopted" by wealthy cousins and later inherited their estates in Kent and Hampshire (on the condition that he changed his family name to "Knight"). Jane mixed with Edward's friends, seeing first-hand the privileged life of the gentry.

These experiences are thought to have shaped much of her fiction.

"Single women have a dreadful propensity for being poor, which is one very strong argument in favour of matrimony..."

Jane Austen in a letter to her unmarried
niece Fanny Knight, 13 March 1816

"So, Lizzy," said he one day, "your sister is crossed in love, I find. I congratulate her. Next to being married, a girl likes to be crossed a little in love now and then."

Mr Bennet on Mr Bingley's seeming rejection
of Jane Bennet,
Pride and Prejudice, 1813

It was over at last, however. The gentlemen did approach.

An illustration from Pride and Prejudice *(Macmillan & Co, 1895)*

"A man who has nothing to do with his own time has no conscience in his intrusion on that of others."

Marianne Dashwood to Elinor Dashwood,
at the sight of Colonel Brandon approaching,
Sense and Sensibility, 1811

"If there is any thing disagreeable going on, men are always sure to get out of it."

Mary Musgrove to Anne Elliot,
Persuasion, 1817

"An engaged woman is always more agreeable than a disengaged. She is satisfied with herself. Her cares are over, and she feels that she may exert all her powers of pleasing without suspicion. All is safe with a lady engaged: no harm can be done."

Henry Crawford on women,
Mansfield Park, 1814

"Adieu to disappointment and spleen. What are young men to rocks and mountains?"

Elizabeth Bennet after being invited to
travel the countryside with Mr and Mrs Gardiner,
Pride and Prejudice, 1813

Jane's writing has spawned countless adaptions of every type: sequel and prequel novels, films, television series and theatrical performances.

The first major film to be produced was the 1940 production of *Pride and Prejudice*, starring Laurence Olivier and Greer Garson.

"I do not think I ever opened a book in my life which had not something to say upon woman's inconstancy. Songs and Proverbs, all talk of woman's fickleness. But perhaps you will say, these were all written by men."

Captain Harville to Anne Elliot,
Persuasion, 1817

"My dear Miss Elizabeth, I have the highest opinion in the world of your excellent judgement in all matters within the scope of your understanding…"

Mr Collins to Elizabeth Bennet,
Pride and Prejudice, 1813

"But Shakespeare one gets acquainted with without knowing how. It is a part of an Englishman's constitution. His thoughts and beauties are so spread abroad that one touches them everywhere; one is intimate with him by instinct. No man of any brain can open at a good part of one of his plays without falling into the flow of his meaning immediately."

Henry Crawford to Edmund Bertram,
Mansfield Park, 1814

Sir John was a sportsman,
Lady Middleton a mother. He
hunted and shot, and she humoured
her children; and these were their
only resources.

Sense and Sensibility, 1811

"Men have had every advantage of us in telling their own story. Education has been theirs in so much higher a degree; the pen has been in their hands."

Anne Elliot to Captain Harville,
Persuasion, 1817

"Mr Tilney!" she exclaimed.

An illustration from Northanger Abbey *(Macmillan & Co, 1897)*

"I have none of the usual inducements of women to marry. Were I to fall in love, indeed, it would be a different thing! But I never have been in love… And, without love, I am sure I should be a fool to change such a situation as mine…

…Fortune I do not want; employment I do not want; consequence I do not want:

I believe few married women
are half as much mistress of
their husband's house as I am of
Hartfield; and never, never could
I expect to be so truly beloved
and important; so always first
and always right in any man's
eyes as I am in my father's."

Emma Woodhouse to Harriet Smith,
Emma, 1815

Jane was extremely close
to her older sister, Cassandra,
and the two exchanged hundreds of
letters. However, after Jane's death,
Cassandra destroyed most of
them – perhaps because they
contained many outspoken and
personal reflections.

The remaining letters still offer
a wonderful and valuable insight
into the author's life.

Woman is fine for her own satisfaction alone. No man will admire her the more, no woman will like her the better for it.

On female vanity,
Northanger Abbey, 1817

"A lady's imagination is very rapid; it jumps from admiration to love, from love to matrimony in a moment."

Mr Darcy to Miss Bingley,
Pride and Prejudice, 1813

Edmund could allow his sister to be the best judge of her own happiness, but he was not pleased that her happiness should centre in a large income; nor could he refrain from often saying to himself, in Mr Rushworth's company — "If this man had not twelve thousand a year, he would be a very stupid fellow."

Mansfield Park, 1814

"But I hate to hear you talking so like a fine gentleman, and as if women were all fine ladies, instead of rational creatures. We none of us expect to be in smooth water all our days."

Anne Elliot to Frederick Wentworth,
Persuasion, 1817

It would be mortifying to the feelings of many ladies, could they be made to understand how little the heart of man is affected by what is costly or new in their attire.

Northanger Abbey, 1817

"

...nothing can be compared to the misery of being bound without love – bound to one, and preferring another; that is a punishment which you do not deserve."

Jane Austen in a letter to her niece Fanny Knight,
warning against a marriage of convenience,
30 November 1814

Jane's sister, Cassandra,
was engaged for a time, but her
fiancé died from yellow fever while
on military service as a chaplain
in the Caribbean.

The two sisters shared the experience
of being unmarried women, which
perhaps explains why they became
such confidants. When not together,
they wrote to each other every
few days.

"**I**f I loved you less, I might be able to talk about it more."

Mr Knightley to Emma Woodhouse,
Emma, 1815

"All the privilege I claim for my own sex (it is not a very enviable one: you need not covet it), is that of loving longest, when existence or when hope is gone!"

Anne Elliot to Captain Harville,
Persuasion, 1817

In 2017, to mark the 200th anniversary of Jane's death, the Bank of England unveiled a new £10 note featuring the author's image.

Austen was the first female author to grace a British bank note, although the honour had already been bestowed on several male authors including William Shakespeare and Charles Dickens.

"I am no longer surprised at your knowing only six accomplished women. I rather wonder now at your knowing any."

Elizabeth Bennet to Mr Darcy,
Pride and Prejudice, 1813

CHAPTER
FIVE

LEISURE & FRIENDSHIP

Jane Austen's characters
are rarely seen working and the
author pays little attention to
their practical responsibilities.

Instead, social visits,
excursions, evening parties and
dances all take centre stage.

"There is nothing I would not do for those who are really my friends. I have no notion of loving people by halves, it is not my nature."

Isabella Thorpe to Catherine Morland,
Northanger Abbey, 1817

"I had a very pleasant evening, however, though you will probably find out that there was no particular reason for it; but I do not think it worth while to wait for enjoyment until there is some real opportunity for it."

Jane Austen in a letter to her sister,
Cassandra, 21 January 1799

When Jane was twenty-five,
her father moved the family to
Bath. He died soon after
and there followed an unsettled
time for Jane, her mother and sister,
who did not have much money.

Eventually, Jane's brother
Edward was able to offer them a
stable home again — a large cottage
on one of his estates in the village
of Chawton, Hampshire.

"

...to sit in the shade on a fine
day, and look upon verdure, is the
most perfect refreshment."

Fanny Price,
Mansfield Park, 1814

"The pleasures of friendship, of unreserved conversation, of similarity of taste and opinions will make good amends for orange wine."

Jane Austen in a letter to her sister,
Cassandra, 20 June 1808

"I am delighted with the book! I should like to spend my whole life reading it. I assure you, if it had not been to meet you, I would not have come away from it for all the world."

Catherine Morland
to her friend Isabella Thorpe,
Northanger Abbey, 1817

"Give him a book, and he will read all day long."

Charles Musgrove on Captain Benwick,
Persuasion, 1817

Sit at her elbow, reading verses.

An illustration from Persuasion *(Macmillan & Co, 1897)*

"**B**usiness, you know, may bring money, but friendship hardly ever does."

Mr Knightley to Jane Fairfax,
Emma, 1815

"

...without music, life would be a blank to me.**"**

Mrs Elton to Emma Woodhouse,
Emma, 1815

Jane began to show signs
of having a serious illness in 1816.
She wrote of being "very poorly"
and of her looks being "black and
white… every wrong colour", in a
letter to her niece, Fanny.

It is now thought Jane was
suffering from Addison's disease
or Hodgkin's Lymphoma.

"We are to have a tiny party here tonight. I hate tiny parties – they force one into constant exertion."

Jane Austen in a letter to her sister, Cassandra, 21 May 1801

"The person, be it gentleman or lady, who has not pleasure in a good novel, must be intolerably stupid."

Henry Tilney to Catherine Morland,
Northanger Abbey, 1817

"I am almost afraid to tell you how my Irish friend and I behaved. Imagine to yourself everything most profligate, and shocking in the way of dancing and sitting down together."

Jane Austen in a letter to her sister,
Cassandra, on meeting Tom Lefroy at a ball
(the man said to be her first love),
9–10 January 1796

Mr Darcy, you must allow me to present
this young lady to you as a very desirable partner.

An illustration from Pride and Prejudice *(Macmillan & Co, 1895)*

To be fond of dancing
was a certain step towards falling
in love...

Pride and Prejudice, 1813

"Here's harmony!" said she; "here's repose! Here's what may leave all painting and all music behind, and what poetry only can attempt to describe! Here's what may tranquillise every care, and lift the heart to rapture! When I look out on such a night as this, I feel as if there could be neither wickedness nor sorrow in the world; and there certainly would be less of both if the sublimity of Nature were more attended to, and people were carried more out of themselves by contemplating such a scene."

Fanny Price,
Mansfield Park, 1814

"

...next week I shall begin my operations on my hat, on which you know my principal hopes of happiness depend."

Jane Austen in a letter to her sister,
Cassandra, 27 October 1798

She put in the feather last night.

An illustration from Sense and Sensibility *(Macmillan & Co, 1896)*

"

...they are much to be pitied who have not been... given a taste for Nature in early life."

Edmund Bertram to Fanny Price,
Mansfield Park, 1814

"Ah! There is nothing like
staying at home, for real comfort."

Mrs Elton to Emma Woodhouse,
Emma, 1815

"It is very, very gratifying to me to know you so intimately. You can hardly think what a pleasure it is to me to have such thorough pictures of your heart. Oh, what a loss it will be when you are married! You are too agreeable in your single state – too agreeable as a niece. I shall hate you when your delicious play of mind is all settled down in conjugal and maternal affections."

Jane Austen in a letter to her niece
Fanny Knight, 20 February 1816

Friendship is certainly
the finest balm for the pangs of
disappointed love.

Northanger Abbey, 1817

CHAPTER

SIX

OBSERVATIONS

Jane Austen's genius lay in her
ability to observe and capture the
minutiae of everyday life.

Her acute insights into human
nature give her writing
timeless appeal — and her musings
are as relevant now as they
ever were.

Let other pens dwell on guilt and misery. I quit such odious subjects as soon as I can, impatient to restore everybody, not greatly in fault themselves, to tolerable comfort, and to have done with all the rest.

Mansfield Park, 1814

In the final months of her life, Jane continued to try to write but abandoned a seventh uncompleted novel when she eventually became bed-ridden.

She was taken to Winchester for treatment and died there on 18 July 1817, at the age of 41.

Jane's unfinished novel
is today known as *Sandition*. Its
dramatic opening line is as follows:

"A gentleman and lady travelling
from Tunbridge towards that part of
the Sussex coast which lies between
Hastings and East Bourne,
being induced by business to quit the
high road, and attempt a very rough
lane, were overturned in toiling
up its long ascent – half rock,
half sand."

"I do not want people to be very agreeable, as it saves me the trouble of liking them a great deal."

Jane Austen in a letter to her sister,
Cassandra, 24 December 1798

"**S**urprizes are foolish things. The pleasure is not enhanced, and the inconvenience is often considerable."

Mr Knightley to Emma Woodhouse,
Emma, 1815

"I think I may boast myself to be, with all possible Vanity, the most unlearned, & uninformed Female who ever dared to be an Authoress.**"**

Jane Austen in a letter to librarian and chaplain,
James Stanier Clarke, 11 December 1815

"Sometimes one is guided by what they say of themselves, and very frequently by what other people say of them, without giving oneself time to deliberate and judge."

Elinor Dashwood to Marianne Dashwood,
Sense and Sensibility, 1811

They sang together.

An illustration from Sense and Sensibility *(Macmillan & Co, 1896)*

Angry people are not always wise.

Pride and Prejudice, 1813

"I cannot help thinking that it is more natural to have flowers grow out of the head than fruit."

Jane Austen in a letter to
her sister, Cassandra, on decorating her hat,
11 June 1799

Seldom, very seldom does complete truth belong to any human disclosure; seldom can it happen that something is not a little disguised, or a little mistaken…

Emma, 1815

"**T**hink only of the past
as its rememberance gives you
pleasure."

Elizabeth Bennet to Mr Darcy,
Pride and Prejudice, 1813

Will you do me the honour of reading that letter?.

An illustration from Pride and Prejudice *(Macmillan & Co, 1895)*

"**H**ad I been in love, I could not have been more wretchedly blind! But vanity, not love, has been my folly…

…On the very beginning of our acquaintance, I have courted prepossession and ignorance, and driven reason away, where either were concerned. Till this moment I never knew myself."

Elizabeth Bennet, after reading Mr Darcy's letter revealing why he broke off the engagement between Jane and Mr Bingham, and why he was in dispute with Mr Wickham, *Pride and Prejudice*, 1813

"Nothing ever fatigues me but doing what I do not like."

Fanny Price,
Mansfield Park, 1814

"

...money can only give happiness where there is nothing else to give it. Beyond a competence, it can afford no real satisfaction, as far as mere self is concerned"

Marianne Dashwood to Elinor Dashwood,
Sense and Sensibility, 1811

Jane was buried
in Winchester Cathedral.
Her memorial stone mentions the
"sweetness of her temper" and the
"extraordinary endowments of her
mind", though neglects to mention
her literary achievements.

In 1872, a plaque was erected next
to her grave to redress this omission
– the inscription begins:
"Jane Austen, known to many
by her writings…"

"I could not sit seriously down to write a serious Romance under any other motive than to save my life, & if it were indispensable for me to keep it up & never relax into laughing at myself or other people, I am sure I should be hung before I had finished the first chapter. No — I must keep my own style & go on in my own way; and though I may never succeed again in that, I am convinced that I should totally fail in any other."

Jane Austen in a letter to librarian and chaplain, James Stanier Clarke, 1 April 1816

Two umbrellas for us.

An illustration from Emma *(Macmillan & Co, 1896)*

"What dreadful hot weather we have! It keeps one in a continual state of inelegance."

Jane Austen in a letter to her sister,
Cassandra, 18 September 1796

"By reading only six hours a-day, I shall gain in the course of a twelve-month a great deal of instruction which I now feel myself to want."

Marianne Dashwood,
Sense and Sensibility, 1811

But strange things may
be generally accounted for if their
cause be fairly searched out.

Northanger Abbey, 1817

" A person may be proud without being vain. Pride relates more to our opinion of ourselves, vanity to what we would have others think of us."

Mary Bennet,
Pride and Prejudice, 1813

After Jane's death,
her sister, Cassandra, wrote,

"I *have* lost a treasure, such a sister,
such a friend as never can have been
surpassed. She was the sun of my
life, the gilder of every pleasure, the
soother of every sorrow; I had not a
thought concealed from her, and it is
as if I had lost a part of myself.
I loved her only too well…"

"I can recollect nothing more to say at present; perhaps breakfast may assist my ideas. I was deceived – my breakfast supplied only two ideas — that the rolls were good and the butter bad."

Jane Austen in a letter to her sister,
Cassandra, 19 June 1799

Jane Austen's fame as
one of the greatest writers in the
English language only began to
grow around the middle of the
nineteenth century.

Her nephew James Edward Austen-
Leigh wrote in his 1869 biography:
"Her reward was not to be the quick
return of the cornfield, but the slow
growth of the tree which is to endure
to another generation".

"But people themselves alter so much, that there is something new to be observed in them for ever."

Elizabeth Bennet,
Pride and Prejudice, 1813